Once Fell From Grace

Once fell from grace
God grants music
Even to the sinfully
Deaf been to the word
Held in subconscious
With an all too
Tangible presence
Light upon me
Center stage
Un-hid from the constraints
Of pride
Kneel.

Shame it
Until the end
People go to
Achieve
Un-holiness
Illuminated all around
Spinning from one
To another vice
Trying to fill souls
With fuel it doesn't
Take away the truth
For the Godless
No redemption.

Independent of the
Light I cannot shine
Anymore in isolation
Cold is overcome
Not by endurance
But the warmth
Of the lord
Shall remain
Burning within me.

These dog days
Are over
A chapter
Filled with love
And loyalty
Distance and truth
Dominus Maximus
Neapolitan extraordinaire
Guardian of my child
You reigned supreme
Perched on a hill
Somewhere else
Some other time
When you kept
Us safe
Silently positioned
Always just right
Everyone will miss you.
But no one like me
Crying like my dog died.

Was no role
Model of good
Behavior
Children look
Up to me
The flaws of history
Control and greed
Fame and fortune
Conquering me
From this parochial
School altar boy
Came rage
From the lies
Of what it meant
To be a good Christian.

What has happened
To this world
Living high on danger
Raising the poverty line
Goes the length of
Our streets begging for
Peace in their belly
Spawns the hunger
Fed by hate
Opposition rally
Protests my freedom
To ask you
For a truce.

Awakened by good
Shall overcome evil
The alarm triumphantly
Sounds reason
That the alleys
Are not shortcuts
To anywhere but
Down.

5 am the word
Awakens me
From sin
Ran away from
God because
Imperfection froze
A state of the heathen
No more time
To be absorbed
In the tug of the world
You get beyond it
With the man upstairs.

The fog is lifted indoors
Between the cracks
It disappears
In sunshine
This place blessed
Beautiful
More good fortune
Than we should ever
Expect to give
Back
To those that really
Need it
Not to impress
But just
Survive.

When the spirit
Enters it feels like
Discovering your
True self
Flesh included
Feels full of might
Yet calm
The touch of
A spiritual hand
Emotionally compels
Me in place.
Of the divine
Awe struck.

Catalyst for drunken
Energy emerges
From some family
Disturbance
Keeps you away
From the table
The longer you wait
The harder it is
To comeback
Is never too late
To compromise desire.

Faith is lodged
In all of us
It remains untapped
Some more hidden than
Others rose from
This baptism
I have been saved
Sometime before death
Is one must hope
All man
The opportunity
For redemption.

Scattered parts
Of lives
That crashed meteorically
All over one another
Emotions were spilled
In expectation
And desire to be
Respected in some ridiculous
Way of spiritual less
Wander for decades
On about your needs
Epic holes in all of us
Love and lust
Swim in and out
Betraying our needs
To fulfill our
Wants
To be emancipated from
The ties that bind us
Assembled unmatched
And passionate
But formidable.

Every so often
The past rings
A bell
Chiming good and bad
News from old stopping points
The grounds of jubilation
Just for life raw
Passionate and damaged
Consumption of wildness
Drunk on liberty
With our souls
Dangling in
The devils hands
Men and women go
To fight wars on each
Other madness of ideology
The land of others
Must matter the same
We all will get along
In a much more
Humane way.

What has happened
Here belongs to
The good of parents
Who experiencing
Faith showed a way
Of hope all the time
We prayed for
Things to get better
They always
Did on the backs
Of ourselves
Holding the
Hand of God
We willingly
Rose from frustration
Captivated in the smell
Of hope.

Different than seeking
Some obscure
Architecture to faith
Or some self-chosen preacher
God let me come
To an understanding
About the imperfection
Of our human condition
Such animals despite
The souls and brains
We need our faith
To not come undone.

What penance for this
World of self created
Delusion of possessions
All the ways
Of hedonism
In the name of God
Only on Sunday
Able to reflect
That disappearing
From here
Becomes do what
You want.

Encrypted on hands
Are the work of God
Underneath the life grime
Soft skin of protection
Is the way we are
Born to caress
Not strangle.

At liberty to tell
Myself be healed
In the hands of God
No time away is too
Long a mercenary
For indiscretion
Submerged in our hands
Release the sin
That we have grasped
Upon ourselves.

Jasmine monkey’s dance
On camels backs
The sun beats down
A bleached alley
Cat prowls
For cover
From kid’s poaching attack
Survival is grim
For those who
Disbelieve
The potential for everyone
Can be unmasked
In rebirth.

Persecute each other
No more un-mercy
Mary mother of me
Pray for us
Now
In this chant
Cast to remember
What it means
To be in the
Light
Warmth resonates
Even in the stark night
Those who obey
Shine bright.

Consequence of healing
In time is that
Open wounds remain on
Some others who
We must heal with love
This was meant
To be prophetic
That driving back
To Christ's sake
We acknowledge our past.

Pockets of faith
Hidden in our
Survival kit
Breed a hike
Back to the
Mainland of God
Our search
For the truth
Was long ago over
When we met
In spirit
On the train of revival.

Chant some philosophy
About independent
Righteousness is for fools
We know the truth
Is larger than man
A street corner
Or gun
Block club streets can’t
Police obedience
Anywhere near
The power of prayers
With hands folded
Much before someone is dead.

Much of us
Don’t want the compromise
Of peace brings
The disappearance of
Value relativism
Leads us to temptation
That we by the decree
Of God
We trust
It is okay to kill whomever
We wish
You a Merry Xmas
In the insane context
Of the birth of democracy.

Spill some of this
Cup of peacefulness
Overflows in
The divine
Inspiration of feeling well
About the world
One thing for certain
It can change
For the good.

Miscues and fumbles
Off sides and procedure
Somewhere in those tree branches
And snow
Life starts warm and safe
the hostility narrows
right inside inhospitable
a saved man
can rest in peace
just like a night bird.

In the heavens
Presume earth
As misfortune
Comes down
Raining on me
Out a window
Become drenched in
A cleansing array
Of kind words
And softness
This time no
Running away from
God is everywhere
That you go to
But easiest to access
In every present
Place.

Why don’t you
Remind me why
We started
All this in
First places
We rose
To the defense
Of each other
Bound before
God witnessed
What this must
Be
You and me.

Somewhere in the summertime
We cleansed the souls
In a less than
Symbolic way
Onto some torment
A wave in the darkness
Worn flat
And placid
He real growth
Under he surface
We recline
In love.

Ancient beast
With wrinkled skin
And pancakes for paws
Drool on your back
From submission
To position
Of full on protect
You guard us fiercely
But quietly
We are amazed
Around you
An aura
Of pure dignity.

You left me a last breath
And a wrestlers embrace
Rock solid we squeezed against
One another dog and man
Until you let go
On double the dose
You are all man
Hard core even on
Two legs you held
Four at bay
A king and soldier
In the same land
Your head rests peacefully
On the thinkers stone
I tell you to let
Go for this world
You are no more
Except all inside me
Your spirit resides
In the phantom bark.

Sinewy the primordial
Tissue that seems
So slave like
Ancient stone cutting
Mass of thickness
The head so large
It defies the features
Of a giant
Big ears and all
It confuses the body
So massive
A ball of dynamo
Seeking to help
One and all
A spirit
Un-racist
Like brothers we
Fall.

I failed to relieve
All my sins
The Lord washed
Away but I
Carried the unnecessary
Guilt in memory
Judging myself
After God
Forgave unworthy
And imperfection
All before
Wanting to begin
Fresh start again
Gasping ends
In the hot water tub
Catching my breath
With God’s forgiveness
I can start to be me.

If you should fall
From grace
And there
Believe you must stay
Remember that forgiveness
Is accessible for
Those who confess to
The crime of human
Imperfection
You can wash your way
To the grace of God
Beholds enormous
Power surges to many
Good outlets.

In this vast
Guilty free
Fall from form
Suddenly shifts
From lonesome cowboy
To ministering
Word of God
take away
all earth sin
cleansed me
to new revival
healing wounds
practiced over time
what comes
over me now
is helping
all mankind to
wash themselves
old gone forever
mystical You
and me forever
live peace.

What do we
Black brother
Know of trust
Each other
Never fully altogether
Renew time
Let's start
Riding the bus
Together want
These barriers down
Altogether forever
Racism can stop
This generation.
Must be bold.

Grateful for thee
Has saved
Me from perpetual
Loneliness dog euthanasia
God bless
Grand old friends
Four legs
And all aware
Mechanically astute
My neo
Watches over me
In death
Remains stronger forever.

So we begin
44 years
Into this life
Breaths taken
And given away
Time evaporates
Our call snores
Rattling endurance
Bitterness rusts away
Leaving strong
The surviving pieces
Have character
Enough to save
The soul
Of the common
Man let go of rage.